Has Anyone Said "I Love You"

Written by Ed Popil AKA Mrs Kasha Davis
Illustrated by Courtney Powitz

Special thanks to **Mr. Davis (Steve Levins)** for continuous loving support, great cooking and book design, **Courtney Powitz** for her fabulous illustrations, **Blackfriars Theatre, Mary Tiballi Hoffman, Danny Hoskins** and **Ben Gonyo** for Imagination Station. A special thank you to **Andy Pratt** for the music for Has Anyone Said "I love you" and **Max** for being the ULTIMATE #soulpup.

Text Copyright © 2021 by Edward Popil Jr
Illustration copyright © 2021 by Courtney Powitz
All rights reserved. No part of this book may be reproduced or transmitted in any form or by any means, electronic or mechanical, including photocopying, recording, or by any information storage and retrieval system, without permission in writing from the author.

Book design is by Steven Levins
For more information visit our web site at www.mrskashadavis.com, email: mrskashadavis@gmail.com.

I love your laughs and smiles.
Even your scratchy face!

The way you always listen
When my thoughts are in a race.

You must embrace the you, you are
To share love far and wide.

Your spirit will be shining,
Shining near and far.

When you feel love blossom,

Now take your love and hold it,

Remember when you share it,

Love grows and grows and grows.

"WHEN WE LOVE OURSELVES, EVERYTHING IS POSSIBLE!" - Mr. & Mrs. Davis

Ed Popil Aka Mrs Kasha Davis

Ed resides in Fairport NY with his loving husband Steve and their dog Max. There is nothing that makes Ed happier than portraying MKD on Imagination Station Live or for TV. Seeing the smiling faces of children of all ages gives him hope that they will see someone who embraces their genuine self and is living a happy, healthy life and that they can too. www.instagram.com/mrskashadavis

Courtney Powitz

Courtney Powitz is thrilled to be making her debut as a picture book illustrator. A graduate of the animation program at the Savannah College of Art and Design, Courtney finds great joy in using her art for self-expression and entertainment. Her love of musical theatre and live performance inspires her to create expressions and characters that are larger than life. She hopes that she too will inspire others to follow their dreams. She sends much love to her family and friends, whose unconditional love and support has helped guide her to where she is today! More of her artwork can be found on social media under the handle @CourtToons.

The idea for this book came from the memories of my youngest sister Nadya Popil. I was one of the oldest siblings of 5 and Mom and Dad needed help with Nadya as they were busy with their careers. It is a JOY of my life to have helped with her as a baby and toddler (she was so cute and a handful!) In my memory we didn't say "I love you" very often if ever as a family. It was meant to be understood but there is power in expressing those words to those you care about and it simply feels good to hear it. I committed to teach Nadya to say I love you every night before bed to our parents and seeing the JOY on their faces told me they truly appreciated hearing it and began to say it back.

If no one has said I love you to YOU today....I do. MAKE IT A GREAT DAY! – Mrs Kasha Davis